A TRAILBLAZER'S GUIDE TO **SUCCESS**

HOW TO AWAKEN YOUR INNER **BOSS**

By

Carla R. Cannon

CANNONPUBLISHING

A TRAILBLAZER'S GUIDE
TO **SUCCESS**

HOW TO AWAKEN
YOUR INNER **BOSS**

By

Carla R. Cannon

CANNON**PUBLISHING**

ALSO BY CARLA R. CANNON

The Power in Waiting

A Single Woman's Focus

Write the Book Already

A Trailblazer State of Mind

The Entrepreneur Blueprint

Turbulence

Burn for Jesus

All available at www.CarlaCannon.com

CANNON PUBLISHING
P.O. Box 1298 Greenville, NC 27835
Office:888-502 2228
Website:www.cannonpublishing.net

ISBN-13: 978-1979569798
ISBN-10: 1979569797

More books by Carla R. Cannon can be purchased at www.CarlaCannon.com and are available for educational, business, or sales promotional use. For booking information for Carla R. Cannon please submit request to Admin@CarlaCannon.com with "Booking Inquiry" in the subject line.

DEDICATION

This book is dedicated to every man, every woman who are tired of playing small and are ready to experience the world in a new and much larger way. Know that you have what it takes to succeed if you will allow yourself to grow from being a person of information to a person of implementation. Remember, as you exceed, reach back and help meet someone else's need. This is how we keep the cycle of success going; by lifting others as we climb.

Table of Contents

INTRODUCTION

Welcome to *A Trailblazer's Guide to SUCCESS: How to Awaken Your Inner Boss!* It is my intention that within the pages of this book you will become enlightened, provoked and awakened to operate on a much bigger level than you are operating currently.

No matter the level of success you have experienced there are always new levels and greater dimensions in which you can accelerate and dominate. However, far too often we as people tend to settle for less than rather than reside in *abundance and overflow.*

Being a woman of color, considered a minority and pretty much operating without a college degree (but totally relying on Holy Spirit, life experiences along with a host of coaches and mentors to guide me,) I am here to share with you how I snatched back my life, shifted my perspective and experienced success not only in my business but every area of my life.

The most important factor of all is that you can too if you are willing to do the work. Know this, nothing changes, if…. nothing…changes….. Again, my friend you have what it takes and with this straight to the point book, know that if I can develop the skills needed to be successful without a college degree, being considered a minority and had (and still have) various odds against me, then all of the excuses you have made up to this present moment no longer matter!

Grab your coffee or tea (or whatever your preference) but leave the blanket because now is not the time to get all cozy.

Truth is you have been comfortable long enough and nothing has ever been birthed out of comfort zones!

Get ready to journey with me as I share with you *A Trailblazer's Guide to Success: How to Awaken Your Inner BOSS!*

Chapter 1

DEFINING SUCCESS
ON YOUR OWN TERMS

Do you currently have a sense of there being more to life but you can't seem to grasp the concept of you actually being able to provide a better life for you and your family? I know what that feels like? I am one who was once on food stamps, living paycheck to paycheck while being a single mother raising my daughter.

I often watched others on television while feeling as if they had some type of special privilege or had some God given ability that I didn't possess. What I later learned is that we all are responsible for our own destiny. We are responsible for whether or not we fail or succeed in life.

Whether you realize it or not we live and die by the decisions we make. Sure, you may be alive physically but are you awakened spiritually? Throughout my journey I have come to the realization that my biggest hindrance was me. We are two people: Who we are currently and who we were created to be. Many of us spend our entire life settling for the person who stares back at us in the mirror, lacking consciousness of the person that lives inside of us who awaits our recognition of their existence.

Truth is, there is no one on the planet more skilled at being you or walking out your life purpose than you. Sadly too many of us waste precious time (which we can never get back) trying to be someone else whom we identify as being successful.

People that may come to your mind may be Oprah Winfrey, Steve Jobs, Bill Gates and beyond but the truth is they too had to fight who they were in order to become who they were created to be. This is what awakening your inner boss is all about.

What you'll learn as you read further is that being a boss is much more than owning your own business but it is about taking ownership for your life and living in a no excuse zone.

Sure, you may have been born into unfortunate circumstances but instead of using that as an excuse why not use it to help others who are stuck in their current condition.

News Flash

Just because you were born there doesn't mean you have to remain there. I was born to parents who were married however, my father struggled with alcohol addiction and my mother was a young wife in her twenties trying to figure it out all on her own. Her mother passed when I was being potty trained therefore, she didn't have the guidance that many of us have access to today.

Unfortunately, I spend much of my life being angry with my mother due to the decisions she made but what set me free was understanding where she was at the time and why she chose the paths she chose.

Whether we realize it or not the decisions we make today will either negatively or positively effect those connected to us. Your reason for awakening your inner boss is so your young daughter, son, niece or nephew and beyond can look at you and say, because you did; I can.

I admire people like Barack and Michelle Obama, Viola Davis and Beyonce. However, I do not want them to be my daughter's role model. I want to be person my daughter looks to and says, Mom, because you did; I learned that I can.

It is pass time for us to get ourselves off of our mind and focus our attention on the real reason why we were placed in the earth. You are not here to simply exist by going to work, pay bills and die. What if I told you that life is much more than what you have been exposed to? I believe it's safe to say this could be a possibility as to why you are not soaring and living the life of your dreams.

The problem with many people is they are waiting for fear to subside before they decide. Fear is crippling many from presenting their true self to the world. Who is your true self? Your true self is who you were to created to be before the foundation of the world. The good book tells us that before the foundation of the earth we had a purpose. It is our assignment and duty to humanity to identify that purpose which in turn will help us better serve the world.

What if I told you that you could make a huge impact in your neighborhood or community? What if it is you who could change the trajectory of your family line? What if you are the one person who could determine whether or not your sons and daughters succeed in life? I am here to tell you that you are.

Whether or not you are a parent, wife, husband or beyond you have people that look to you for advice whether they come to you directly or not. No matter who you are, where you have been or even if you are leading in a positive or negative manner, you are either teaching others by the life you live what to do or what not to do.

It is my heart's desire and full intention to provide you with tools on how to live the life of your dreams and to do so in an authentic and unapologetic manner. Whether this is the first book you have read or mine or not please open your heart and mind by allowing me to share further wisdom with you on how to achieve success in your life.

Before we go any further, I encourage you to grab a piece of paper or if you are a technology driven person grab your phone and go to the notes section and write this down: \

My Definition of Success

Throughout my six years of entrepreneurship I've learned that many are seeking something that they have yet defined. Success is more than some shallow desire. Success is also more than money, cars, power and entitlement. Success is what keeps you in your place of peace. I believe this is what many desire more than anything in life.

As you watch the news you learn of celebrities and leaders committing suicide while living in million dollar homes and more but yet found life to not be worth living.

We all are familiar with Whitney Houston; one of the world's greatest voices. Or perhaps Robin Williams who made the world laugh with his great impersonations. Elvis Presley, who was known as the King of Rock and Roll. Michael Jackson, known as the King of Pop. According to the society these individuals were the epitome of success but I believe due to the way things ended for them there was something they each were seeking that money couldn't seem to buy: PEACE.

I contemplated on including this in the book but after careful consideration I learned these are the individuals many of us ordinary people look to and sadly often compare ourselves to. Why am I sharing this? Because I want you to identify what success looks like for you and not base it on material things or heights others have reached.

In life it is all about reaching your level of greatness; not others. One thing that keeps me humbled and in a peaceful state is maintaining a heart of gratitude no matter the opposition I may be facing at a particular time in my life.

Did you know that over 350 million people either have suffered or currently suffer with depression? Depression is a state of feeling sad. Other definitions include feelings of hopelessness or a reduction in activity, amount, quality or force.

Sadly, many suffer from depression but are unaware of it. Although I have never been clinically diagnosed as being depressed but I have suffered from severe feelings of hopelessness and beyond. There were times in my life where I laid in my bed for days at a time crying and feeling as if my life was out of control and beyond recovery.

There was also a time in which I attempted suicide by taking a full body of pills. It is only by the grace of God that I am still here today because depression once had me bound because I felt as if I was exactly who others had identified me as due to how my life started out.

But one day it was as if I had a subconscious conversation with my future self. I saw myself out of my current dilemma. I smelled fresh air, saw new faces and felt a peace that was beyond description. It was in that moment that I signed the divorce papers with self-pity and made a cognizant decision to snatch back my life.

Now please know that my current situation remained the same but in that moment my mind had changed. That is what determines whether or not you will be successful in life. If you can see yourself beyond your current condition then you have the power to live through that current season of your life.

Truth is, life happens to all of us but it is our response to it that determines our destiny. My reason for sharing this is to show you that you do not have to sit back and allow life to happen to you but you can do something about the things that have happened in your life.

You can choose to feel sorry for yourself or you can choose to outlive your current story. Just because your path started out a particular way doesn't mean it has to remain the way it is.

The purpose of this book is to unfold strategies combined with life principles that will help you enter into a place of peace that will lead you to *your* definition of success.

By now it is my hope that you have defined what success looks like for you instead of comparing your life to that of others which will rob you of your success.

Get ready as we dive in to activate your inner BOSS!

Chapter 2

DEFINITION OF A BOSS

Webster's Dictionary defines a "boss" as a person who exercises control or authority; *specifically*: one who directs or supervises workers. I define a boss as someone who is clear of their purpose, unapologetically embraces and operates in it and helps lead and activate others along the way.

I define success as a:

Bold Servant Who
Optimistically Pursues Purpose in a
Strategic & Unapologetic Manner While Uplifting Their
Savior

That's my definition of a BOSS. Funny thing is that was released to me while in prayer and I was asking God why He had me teaching from the aspect of being a boss being that many had been using that term to mean things I did not agree with.

His response was that He wanted to use me in the earth to redefine it. Being a boss is much more than about owning a business but it is a mindset.

Characteristics of a boss include one who operates in character, integrity, resilience and humility. Being a boss doesn't mean you are above anyone but you recognize that you were put on earth to serve and you serve in excellence, humility and authenticity while doing so unapologetically.

Another definition of a boss is someone (man or woman) who is (1) Clear of their purpose, (2) Unapologetically embraces and operates in it (3) Helps lead and activate others along the way!

My question to you today is, do you consider yourself a boss? Many have embraced this word and tied it to the amount of revenue they bring in and use it as a determining factor to calculate their worth.

Truth is we are all in the process of *becoming* (who we were created to be) so whether you are in the planning phase of launching your business, or still in the discovery phase of identifying your purpose; either way you are still a boss! Know this, the work of Jesus has already been done in Heaven. We are simply working diligently to get our natural to line up with our supernatural. So you are not a *Boss in the Making*, but you already possess the characteristics of a true boss they simply haven't been awakened yet!

One of my goals within the pages of this book is to help you up-level your life by first up-leveling your language and changing your perspective. Guess what else? Who you surround yourself with is detrimental in relation to how you speak and view life.

A real boss not only leads the pack but he or she joins arms with other bosses in an effort to create maximum impact.

Who is your *boss-hero*? Your *boss-hero* may be your mother because you watched her press forward and provide for you and your siblings on a daily basis making much out of a little, and she did so without complaining while putting herself through school and managing to not go insane in the process! Now that indeed sister girl or brother man, is a true *boss!*

Or perhaps your *boss-hero* is a woman like Oprah Winfrey who started from the bottom where her grandmother was a maid and had positioned and prepared Oprah to follow in her footsteps. But Oprah being a woman who wanted and desired more out of life, knew television was her calling therefore, she pursued a career in broadcasting which led to her hosting her very own internationally popular talk show from 1986 to 2011 (which became the #1 talk show in America.) She went on to be an actress, philanthropist, publisher (Oprah Magazine) and producer of various movies and sitcoms as well as establishing her very own network (Oprah Winfrey Network known as OWN.) She did all of this in the midst of the various odds she faced while in the process of becoming. Oprah has also been identified as the first African American billionaire.

Talk about a true boss!!!!! Now guess what? Although it was her success that many tend to highlight what really makes Oprah a boss is the many failures she experienced throughout this process in which I'm sure her BFF Gayle King was there to witness and perhaps it was her prayers that helped push Oprah to her next level so to the point that Oprah gave Gayle a million dollars.

Who knew this kind gesture and exchange of currency between Oprah and Gayle would cause the world to go up in an uproar? Many went on blogs and various social media outlets making various accusations about Oprah and Gayle's sisterly relationship. I personally had a different perspective. While everyone else saw Oprah on television appearing to make *boss* moves, I believe it was Gayle that nurtured and coached Oprah back to life each time she was tempted to give up or when things got harder as Oprah approached her next level of victory.

Every boss needs a midwife because it takes a boss to birth a boss. Remember that!

CALL TO ACTION:

Take a moment to dig deep and ask yourself the following questions.

How often do you sit back and watch other boss men or women operate in their purpose while you fail to operate in your true, authentic power?

□ Always   □ Occasionally   □ Never

What are three things you can do differently today to awaken your inner boss?

1. _____

2. _____

3. _____

In what ways have you downplayed your vision or dream?

_____

_____

_____

_____

_____

_____

How passionate are you about your life?

Have you lost your fire?

Have you lost your drive/motivation?

What can you do today to reignite the fire in your life?

_____

_____

_____

_____

_____

_____

_____

_____

_____

Chapter 3

IDENTIFYING POWER PARTNERS

Just as Oprah has Gayle, Thelma had Louise, Batman had Robin and Elizabeth and Mary, you too will need a power partner to experience life with. One who will push you forward when you want to give up, one who will remind you of why you started when pursuing your dreams no longer seem worth it. One who will not criticize you when you have weak moments but will allow you to be human and make mistakes and then not throw them in your face.

Your power partner(s) is someone who sees what others rarely see. They see and know the *real* you a part from your brand, successful endeavors; etc. They see the *real* you when you fail. They see the real *you* that balls up in a fetal position the first time you read something unpleasant that a critic posted of you on social media.

Your power partner is someone who knows the real you yet they still love you. They will cover your weaknesses and protect you at all cost. In your most vulnerable moments they will love and coach you through your valley/wilderness experiences and even walk with you via public appearances when need be.

Power partner(s) are not fans but they are your true friends. Fans are there and rooting for you when all is well. But real friends will stick closer than a brother when it all falls apart.

13

Often times in my life I have mistaken fans for friends. Being a woman who grew up battling rejection and wrestling with feelings of abandonment and anyone who showed me love or celebrated me I seemed to latch on to. It wasn't until I learned the importance of self-love and disconnected from desperation that I learned that they really didn't love me, they loved what I represented, where I was headed and doors of opportunity I could open for them.

Now that my friend was the hard part: learning the truth about individuals in your circle yet being too afraid to release them and walk alone (for a season.) Sadly, we mistaken power partners for people who are celebrating us publically because of our success. But what happens when your money runs out and you have to file bankruptcy, or what happens when it's your kid in the news and you have to face the public? What happens when it's your marriage that falls apart?

As you grow, develop and pursue a path of purpose that will leave a legacy behind for your family, it is important to be able to identify your power partners and give everyone else a back seat. Now, giving them a back seat doesn't mean you cut them off. It just means there are only a select few that can enter into the holy of holies with you.

Just as the greatest man who ever walked this earth had a team of twelve that accompanied him, he only became intimate with three. Now is the time to identify your power partners and hold them close, giving them access to parts of you they can be trusted with. Everyone can't handle your vulnerabilities.

Everyone can't handle your *entire* truth. Therefore, be careful in whom you connect and share with. Now, I am not saying this for you to become suspicious but for you to operate cautiously in the area of relationships and connections.

World renowned leader, Bishop T.D. Jakes says there are (3) areas in which we identify people: confidantes, constituents, comrades. Confidants are those in which you share with intimately, you trust them, they are your power partners. This relationship is not one sided. You share intimate/vulnerable details of your life with them just as they do with you. These are the ones in which you can be transparent and vulnerable with and they won't use what you share against you.

If you have three in a lifetime that you can really trust you have done extremely well. This will be your smallest category. If you go up, they are with you. If you go down, or get stuck, they are with you! Whether people love or hate you, they are with you and whether you are broke or rich they still stick by you!

Bishop Jakes sums it up by saying, *"These are the people in which you are so comfortable with that when around them you can behave as if you are by yourself."* My God! What a power partner! With your confidants, this is a *masks off zone.* Meaning while I'm in the presence of my confidants I don't have to be The Trailblazer; I can just be Carla.

He goes on to say that confidantes are people who weep when you weep and rejoice when you rejoice. He says when you receive good news and go to share it with your *friends,* stop celebrating for a moment to see who is actually celebrating with you. Bishop Jakes continues by saying, *"If you share good news and they are not celebrating with you, turn around and walk right back out the room!"*

I have experienced this first hand and I must admit it hurt me to my core. I can't recall what had happened but I do recall being very happy about it and I went to share it with what I thought was four of my best girlfriends. When I went to share the news we were all on a conference line and believe it or not when I got finished sharing the good news I had received you could literally hear a pen drop on the phone. Not *one* of my four girlfriends said a single word. I didn't receive an, *"Oh Carla that is great!"* *"I am so happy for you!"* Not even a *"When are we going to celebrate?"* I guess I would have been happier if they would have at least acted like or pretended to be happy for me. But that moment was destined to happen and it changed my life forever.

Here I was sharing great news with a group of women who I had been praying for, carrying in my spirit daily, coaching and mentoring, taking with me on the road as new opportunities arose in my life and now not *one* of them were happy for me. In my mind we were like the women off of the novel turned movie, Waiting to Exhale. Now I'm not sure who was who but you couldn't tell me that we weren't Robin, Savannah, Gloria and Bernadine! We had cried together plenty of times but when my moment to rejoice came I was the only one rejoicing.

I remember this piercing my soul and although it was some time ago I have never forgotten it. That one moment changed my relationship with those four women forever. Why am I

16

sharing this? Some of you are holding on to people you have known for years and when you really examine and evaluate the friendship all you have are *all these years*. In order to enter into my *next*, I had to accept what God was showing me *now* about those who walked the closest with me. What I wasn't prepared for was the next season of my life that I'd have to walk alone. It was painful but it was worth it and God sent a true sister, who has proven to be confidante for real in my life who literally helped carry me through that season. He did this for me and He will do the same thing for you.

Often times we hold on to friendships we know are over out of fear of being alone. But I encourage you to release that space so the new, authentic power partners God has for you can enter into your life.

Next are constituents: They are with the cause. They stand for what you stand for but not necessarily are standing with you. They will confuse you because they will appear to be a confidante but they are only there because of the cause and not because of you! Their attraction is the mission and it is important to know why they are with you. They are there only for their personal agenda and will leave you if another opportunity comes that appears to be able to bring them closer to their destination. The major difference between confidantes and constituents is their motive. They do the same thing: both stand with you, fighting the good fight but one of them will leave you when the road gets tough; these my friend are constituents.

Bishop Jakes continues to say that we can't try to protect ourselves by having a room full of confidantes. We must be able to work with people who will come and go. This is a true sign of maturity. Love them when they come and love them when they leave.

The final category is comrades. They are not for you or for what you are for but they are against what you are against. They will team up with you to fight a greater enemy. But don't be confused by their associations because they are only with you until you experience victory. Don't be upset when your constituents and comrades leave; both are necessary for a season but your loyalty must lie with your confidantes.

Now that you have all of this information, who are your power partners? In the professional world, a power partner is defined as a group of businesses that band together to use and promote the products of the other businesses in the group. There is an old saying; *"No Man is an Island."* No one can do it alone in the business world. With this being said, power partners are those who will promote you and your movement and vice versa.

Now what I don't want you to do is beat yourself up if you have yet to connect with power partners. Focus your attention on *becoming* a power partner and you will in return *attract* power partners.

Now, that we have crossed that bridge, let's talk about the Law of Attraction. I believe many have a misconception of what it is and how it really works.

The **Law of Attraction** is the name given to the maxim "like attracts like" which in New Thought philosophy is used to sum up the idea that by focusing on positive or negative thoughts a person brings positive or negative experiences into their life.

Simply put, we attract what we *are* not what we desire. If you are tired of attracting people who are sucking the life out of you, draining you of all of your energy, commit to serving others and becoming what you desire to attract.

I hear countless stories of what we would identify as *bad* connections. I honestly believe there really is no such thing. My philosophy is that regardless of the experience or the individual in which we encounter, people enter into our lives (whether seasonal or for a life time) to actually teach us more about ourselves.

Therefore, if you are in an abusive relationship currently that is a direct indication of how you feel and view yourself. If you continue to attract business partners with poor morals, or lack an authentic value system it is simply a reflection of what really resides on the inside of us.

In order to attract power players into your life you must first become a power person yourself. Rid yourself of excuses, honor your word (by keeping it), extend grace and love, and have pure intentions (motives) when connecting with others.

Sadly, we live in a society where so many are out for what they can get. I have had so many people desire to connect with me not because they like who I am as a person but for a.) What I represent or b.) What I can (or so they feel) offer them.

I admit this is an extremely painful reality; however, it is life and the world we live in. During various teachings and trainings I encourage my audience to be cautious of people but not suspicious.

Being cautious enables you to guard your space and view the connection objectively without holding them responsible for past hurts and disappointments. Being cautious simply means you do your best to avoid being hurt, used or abused by the individual. Now being truthful, some pains in life are simply unavoidable for this is how we learn.

We learn what we will and will not accept based on how it makes us feel and you must set the standard and establish boundaries and what I call *non-negotiables* prior to the arrival of those you desire to attract.

Non-negotiables are those things that are not up for discussion or modification. Non-negotiables are contingent upon an individuals' core values. What you will and will not accept can only be determined by you. In the book, The Woman Code, Sophia Nelson says that we teach others how to treat us by how we treat them as well as by identifying what we will and will not accept.

I totally agree with this concept. Because if I am offering someone honesty as well as my time and they continue to lie and treat me as an afterthought their actions fall in my category of *non-negotiables*.

Once I have identified the behavior and continue to accept it, I then have to conduct a self-evaluation and investigate why I accepted this behavior. Truth of the matter is in order to be a boss one must have a healthy perspective of themselves. Who you are is a reflection of what you do.

I disagree that we are what we repeatedly do. For me it is the spiritual concept behind it because often times we can do things that really aren't a reflection of who we are. Being a woman of transparency there were times in my life where I wasn't always honest, operated with integrity or knew my true value. Therefore, I often did things that did not display who Carla really was. Now, does your actions cause people to form an opinion of you? Absolutely! I can recall women such as Tami Roman and Evelyn Lozada from VH1's hit television series, Basketball Wives hosted by Shaunie O'Neal. Both of these ladies hit the scenes swinging (and I do mean this figuratively.) They appeared to be what Being Mary Jane calls an "Angry Black Woman."

However, over time they assessed their behavior and got to the root of their issues and learned that it was past hurts and life experiences that left them bitter, angry and with what we would call anger management issues.

If you fast forward over time we have had the opportunity to witness these two beautiful women grow and evolve into more respectable women by controlling their anger, thinking before they speak; etc.

I can recall on several occasions how both women would mention (on the TV show) how they were not the way the world (TV viewers) perceived them to be. But the truth is they were judged by their actions.

They came on the scene fighting, cursing and appearing to be extremely argumentative and again as, "Angry Black Women," therefore, that label became attached to them. However, since then Evelyn Lozada has appeared on the hit TV show that appears on OWN (Oprah Winfrey Network), Iyanla Fix My Life and with the help of Motivational Speaker and Relationship Expert, Iyanla Vanzant was able to get to the core of her issues which really came down to fear and hurt.

Tami Roman also began to work on herself and becoming a better role model for her daughter as well as women in general. Now, are these women perfect? Absolutely, none of us are. Do they still have a lot of work to do? Sure! But who doesn't? The point I'm making is how their actions defined how others viewed them.

The same is true for you and I. We must be mindful of the things we say and do because other people's perspective is their reality. Now, I am not saying you must live for others but what I am saying is that in true essence we often times do and say things that don't properly display the true essence of who we are at our core.

Therefore, in attracting power players we must be willing to do the work by dealing with (not ignoring) our issues.

Characteristics of a Power Partner

1. They face their fears head on

2. They allow nothing or no one to cripple them.

3. They own their truth and are un-apologetic about it

4. They know their value and are not afraid to charge what they are worth.

5. They do not fear failing but understand it is a prerequisite for succeeding.

6. They know what they want out of life and are not afraid to go after it.

7. They show up BIG on a daily basis despite what they may be facing personally.

8. They have committed to doing their work and in return extend grace to others.

9. They think optimistically rather than pessimistically.

10. They dream with their eyes wide open!

CALL TO ACTION:

Take a moment to dig deep and ask yourself the following questions.

The key to successfully moving forward is responding truthfully.

Remember: It is impossible to conquer what you are unwilling to confront and it is impossible to confront what you are unwilling to identify.

1.) Acknowledge where you are currently.
Currently I am_____.

2.) How did you arrive here?
I arrived here by_____.

3.) What are the necessary steps needed to transform your life now.
In order to transform my life I need
to_____

_____

_____

_____

_____

_____.

What is one thing you can do differently today that can change the dynamics of your life?

_____

Who do you need to disconnect from today that is hindering you from presenting your best self to the world?

_____

Identify what you fear most about relationships and then commit to doing the work to overcoming that fear; what I call one of the 5 internal fires we battle daily (along with intimidation, busyness, worry, anxiety and insecurity.)

_____

_____

_____

_____

_____

_____

_____

_____

_____

Chapter 4

TOP 10 RULES FOR SUCCESS

I absolutely love You Tube videos! I admit, I am addicted! Anything you want to learn is on either Google or You Tube. Seriously, it is. Don't believe me, try it! One day as I was seeing what was new I came across a series of videos where some of today's renowned speakers, actors/actresses, (both present and who have passed on) and more shared their "Top 10 Rules for Success."

They featured tips from the late great Maya Angelou, Morgan Freeman, Joel Osteen, Jack Canfield, Steve Harvey, Steve Jobs, Michael Jordan, Steven Spielberg, Nick Vujicic, Jim Rohn, Warren Buffett, Oprah Winfrey and many more!

As I was watching various videos this is what honestly prompted me to write a book entitled, *A Trailblazer's Guide to Success*. As I listened to many of these *celebrities* share their *Top 10 Rules for Success*, I in turn thought it would be awesome to share mine with you as well.

Now, I am by no means saying I am on the same level as the individuals I have mentioned above, however, I will declare that I am well on my way. Too often in life we operate from an *Us VS Them* perspective and the only difference between you and I and *celebrities* is opportunity.

In life we all have the same level of advantages/opportunities whether you were born in one of the poorest countries in the world, grew up not knowing who your biological parents were, or even if you were a high school or college dropout or whatever excuse we use as to why our lives is the way it is.

We must become masters of our lives knowing that it doesn't matter how we start or enter into this world. What matters is what we do and the mark we leave in this world before we exit it. Because truthfully, as humans we never like to think about our expiration date. But guess what? Whether you like to think about it or not, we all have one.

Honestly, none of us know when we will take our last breath. That mother who kissed her baby goodbye as she went away to college, never knew it would be her child's college campus that was invaded by a sniper.

When you kiss your spouse goodbye in the morning while saying, "Have a great day honey!" You never knew a few hours later or even moments later you would receive a knock on your door from the Sheriff's Department. telling you that your spouse was killed in a Motor Vehicle Accident.

The point I am making is that life is short and we must make an intelligent decision today not to just enjoy it but to make it count! What we do today, affects our tomorrow. We can choose to engage in topics and activities that really do not matter. Or we can choose to focus on our life assignment and be committed to dig deeper into our purpose on a daily basis.

Whatever you choose is completely up to you!

I'd like to make my dash count. Your dash is what comes after your birthdate. For example, I was born on June 22, 1984 therefore, it would read like this: "June 22, 1984 -" Do you see that dash in the middle? That will be filled with however I chose to spend my life. Same applies to you.

In life you have the opportunity to do something great for others but the key to awakening your inner boss is to 1.) Identify why you were born 2.) Master the task 3.) Share your gift with the world.

Refuse to compare your process, gifts or even your level of intelligence to others. If there is a skill you don't know but desire to, go learn it! If there is a certain amount of money you want to make by this year's end, go strategize a plan and implement it that will enable you to earn it!

Now, for my Top 10 Rules for SUCCESS. Are you ready? I encourage you to tweet these one by one on Twitter and be sure to tag me in @CarlaRCannon. You can also share nuggets from this book by using the hashtag #bossmoves

1. **Have Courage to Believe in Yourself** - Never allow previous failures to prevent you from trying again. Every successful person failed in various areas before finding their *sweet spot*. Therefore, use the disappointment as ammunition to go harder after purpose!

2. **Show up BIG Daily-** It's important that we deal with our insecurities, anxieties, fear, bad habits; etc. in private. Often times what we don't realize is those things show up with us each time we are present. Refuse to be a public success yet a hot mess privately. Only dealing with your issues privately causes you to show up BIG in public!

3. **Be Clear on Your Vision & Intention-** In life you must have a direct aim as it relates to 1.) Who do you want to become? 2.) Where do you desire to go? 3.) What will it take for you to get there? Answering these three questions are essential to intentional living. In order to be successful in life one must give each day direction by partaking in tasks only that will lead them closer to their destiny.

4. **Understand the Power of "NO."-** If you are going to succeed in your life you must become comfortable with saying "No." Not every opportunity is the opportunity for you. Some people want to appear to have it all and desire to have it all therefore, they accept every opportunity presented to them. I disagree with this totally. If it does not help increase your bottom line by bringing you closer to your ultimate vision (your dream) then you must say, "No!" Saying "No," may hurt at first but once you get comfortable with it, it'll become easier and you will later see that you reserved your energy for more purposeful activities.

5. **Don't Be Anxious/Embrace Your Process-** This is the part where I see many have a hard time. Everyone wants to make it and truth is I am still not clear on what the definition of making it really is. We are all in the process of becoming who we were originally created to be therefore, we must learn to embrace our process and spend our days preparing for our moment. So what if Oprah never calls? So what if they never choose your product to invest in on Shark Tank? You must know that delayed doesn't mean denied. Your story is still being written therefore, keep pressing!

6. **Define What SUCCESS Means to You-** Before you set out to pursue your dreams/goals and position yourself to be able to dream with your eyes wide open, I encourage you to take time to define what success means to you. Because if you don't define it now for yourself, someone else will define it for you. Many get caught up into thinking success is all about material possessions. I know plenty of people who have less than what others have but they have one thing many lack and desire. Guess what that is? PEACE. So, take a moment and define what success looks like, feels like and is for YOU.

7. **Marry Your Vision-** You must be in this thing for the long haul. Point blank PERIOD! It's time out for dating the idea of becoming an entrepreneur. But you must explore the possibilities of your dreams coming true because many are living out their dream daily as

you waste time playing small and refusing to show up BIG everyday of your life. Marry your vision and get rid of Plan B! When you rid yourself of various options Plan A has no choice but to work.

8. **Be Resilient. Persistent & Consistent-** In life you will experience heartbreaks, challenges and setbacks, but your ability to bounce back is a key determining factor for your success. Evaluating how quickly you overcome challenges, where you choose to place your focus: on the problem or the solution, who you fill your circle with and who you choose to marry or partner with all play a major part in your success. Develop a predetermined mindset and refuse to lose!

9. **Connect with Power Players-** In life you are identified by who you are connected with. If you hang out with losers, you will be labeled as a loser. If you hang out with thieves and liars that is how you will be identified. Connecting with power players are essential to your development which will in turn lead to a life full of success (love, peace and happiness/joy.) Reason being is because power players are individuals who are 100% in your corner, they have zero time to hate on you because they are fully confident and comfortable operating in their own lane but they are also committed to your success. Power players are not envious of your success. Find people who can celebrate with you and then my friend you may be on to something great!

10. **Hire a Coach/Mentor-** In life you can not accomplish your dreams on your own. You weren't designed to. The dreams/vision God placed within you was designed with purpose partners in mind. You do not have what it takes to succeed all on your own. This is why I say get rid of "Self-Made" and declare that you are "God-Made" because first of all He is your #1 coach. He also has earthly vessels in which you can partner with to learn that in which you do not know. My motto is nothing changes, if nothing changes.

Lastly, in hiring a coach/mentor know that it doesn't mean you are buying a new friend or pal. Your coach is there to primarily do four things: (1) Stretch you (Here they will *gut* you- Help you get rid of things that are hindering you from developing and maintaining momentum and *not* telling you what you want to hear. They will also help *cut* you by helping you peel off layers of regret, defeat and denial.

Lastly, they help *birth* you into your destiny! They do not pretend opposition doesn't exist but what they do is assist you on how to remain resilient while providing strategies on how you can overcome *anything* life may throw at you! (2) help you face your fears, (3) Overcome your anxieties, and (4) present the best version of yourself to the world on a daily basis!

A *real* coach acts as a spiritual mid-wife (whether male or female) and their main objective is to cause you to become introduced to the person you never thought you could be! That my friend is the true purpose of a coach!

BONUS:

Understanding the Power of FOCUS-

F.O.C.U.S. stands for the following:

Follow
One
Course
Until
Successful

In my bestselling book, *The Entrepreneur Blueprint: How to Develop Your Darkest Storms into a Thriving Business*, in Chapter 5 I share the danger of chasing more than one rabbit (dream/goal/task at a time.) One of the reasons many aspiring entrepreneurs fail is due to a lack of focus.

DIVIDED FOCUS = NO FOCUS

Ben Tankard shares in his book, The Full Tank Life: Fuel Your Dreams, Ignite Your Destiny the following formula which compliments the formula I mentioned above.

FOCUS + MASTERY= EXPANSION

Media Mogul, Tyler Perry encourages both aspiring and emerging entrepreneurs to focus on one thing and master it until completion. I call it birthing it, nursing it and raising it up until you accumulate enough capital for it to stand on its own. Then, head over to the next goal and repeat the process!

Chapter 5

KEYS TO AWAKEN YOUR INNER BOSS

There is a boss that is within each and every one of us which includes an ability to win in life and become the best version of who we were created to be.

Often times many settle for where they are and how things are because they have yet to meet someone who can activate greatness within them that has been there all the while.

Activation is a powerful thing and it simply means to make active.

Many have untapped potential dwelling on the inside of them that remains there until it is awakened. Your inner boss can be awakened from hearing the right message, reading the right material (books; etc.), through spiritual encounter and beyond.

However, there are no excuses when it comes to life and it is no coincidence that you are reading this book at this particular time in your life. View this book as a tool of impartation or awakening to introduce you to the person you have been seeking all the while: your *true* self.

Often times we gain information yet never tap into the revelation behind it which in turn never leads us to implementation, but rather a place called *stuck* which is exactly where we do not desire to be.

Below are ten ways to awaken your inner boss:

1. **Be Open to Criticism and Feedback-** Everyone is not your enemy and you need people around you who will tell you the truth; not what you want to hear and you my friend must be able to handle it. Entrepreneurship is not for the faint hearted.

2. **Study/Perfect Your Craft-** Know your message inside/out to the point that you can create vivid pictures and storylines with the words you use that leave your audience in awe of your presentation. This enables you to create an experience in the midst of sharing your story or pearls of wisdom which have afforded you the various opportunities and success in life.

3. **Identify Your Target Market-** Let's be clear: You are not called to serve everyone. Find out who you feel called to and fill your calendar with serving individuals of that caliber.

4. **Master Your Message-** Although you may offer similar products or services as other professionals in your field, your key to standing out in a crowded market is learning and executing the necessary skill of effectively sharing your story. Sure you may have a product in which a customer could very well go and purchase from another coach but the number one connecting factor between you and your audience (prospects and customers) is your compelling story.

Master it, package it then monetize it! This is what I call *packaging your brilliance!*

5. **Choose to be Proactive Rather Than Reactive-** If you and I go through life reacting to situations around us we will never succeed. The key is to respond versus react. A reaction is simply something you and I would do on impulse. A response rather is a more educated and settled reply to a matter. Make a decision today to no longer react to the things that are happening around you but pick and choose what you will respond to. There is a difference!

6. **Never Be Afraid of Failing-** All failure is are growth moments. The more you learn and fail the more you'll develop and master your craft.

7. **Value TIME -** Rid yourself of people who do not value time. You also want to become someone who values time. Give yourself enough time to show up to designated places and appointments early (if you are on time you are actually late. Remember you have to think like a boss not an employee!) We all have 24 hours in a day but it's up to us how we spend it.

8. **Remove Doubt-** You are capable, worthy and deserving to accomplish and achieve all you desire out of life.

9. **Develop Discipline in Five Key Areas of Your Life:** (1) Spiritual- You must believe in a higher being.

There is just no way to think you can make it out here on your own. (2) Mental- In life you must develop mental toughness. This is how you think and resolve challenges that arise in life. If you are defeated in your mind, you will be defeated in life. (3) Physical- It's important that you take care of your physical body for in doing so you will be able to do your best work and accomplish your dreams while being in the best shape of your life. When you feel great you can do great things! (4) Relational- You must learn how to get along with others. Success in life has a lot to do with the relationships we develop and nurture. No wonder they say it's lonely at the top. If that's the case why are so many people in such a hurry to get there? Because we have bought into the idea of a false sense of success. You can be cash poor, but relationship wealthy; now I'm not saying that is the road you want to take, but hopefully you get my point. (5) Financial- Many are on a path to financial freedom and that doesn't mean that you have to become a millionaire. Only you can define what being financially free looks like to you. I encourage you to start by spending less than you make and sowing ten percent to charity or your local church. No need to keep up with the Joneses, they are dead broke!

10. **Talk To Your Future Self Daily-** One way to refrain from getting stuck where you are is to keep your vision in front of yourself daily as you have a conversation about what is to come. Always speak in present tense.

While in the process of losing the weight, look yourself in the mirror and brag on your flat stomach. It doesn't matter that you still have a muffin top or that your thighs rub together. This exercise is you talking to your future self in an effort to not get stuck where you are! Always speak in present tense while committing to the work and before you know transformation will take place literally before your eyes.

CALL TO ACTION

After reading this, what do you commit to doing differently and how do you intend to apply the above principles to your life now?

_____

_____

_____

_____

_____

_____

_____

_____

_____

_____

_____

_____

Chapter 6

LIVING YOUR DREAM LIFE

I have been afforded the opportunity to travel across the country activating men and women into purpose. The core message that I find myself sharing is that living the life of our dreams is possible however, it will cost us.

Although this is not a popular message it holds to be true. This is why you can't get caught up in the lives of others as you scroll through your social media pages and everyone appears to be winning in life.

Social media allows people to put whatever person or perception (or deception rather) that they want others to believe as it relates to who they are and the life they live. While some of what they share may be true, while displaying their success not many expose what happens behind the scenes of their life.

I travel as a transformational speaker therefore, I may post pics of me in and out of airports or speaking or selfies with supporters (I despise the word *fans*) but I also share pics of my prayer closet or rituals of how I prepare spiritually.

When you commit to being a Kingdom BOSS man or woman you will encounter spiritual warfare however, it is your relationship with God that will sustain you.

I've noticed a lot of people talk about their faith but very few walk it out daily. Walking out your faith daily will display how well you handle opposition and disappointments.

Experiencing turbulence is a part of the process but it will only hinder you if you allow it. I talk in depth about overcoming adversity in my book, *Turbulence* and I recommend you read it if you are currently in a storm that seems there is no way out.

This my friend is a part of living your dream. You must be willing to take on all that comes with it. There will be good days and there will be challenging ones but how you handle them determines the outcome of your destiny.

There are many people I admire and look up to and although I admire their work ethics and success I learn more about their character as I study their *behind the scene* story of how the handle and overcame adversity.

Steve Harvey experienced homelessness and divorce

Tony Robbins experienced poverty

Oprah Winfrey experienced sexual abuse

Robin Roberts experienced sickness

Joyce Meyer experienced sexual, mental and verbal abuse from her father

T.D. Jakes experienced poverty and the death of his mother

Sarah Jakes experienced teenage pregnancy and low self esteem

R&B Singer Monica experienced heartbreak and witnessed her ex-boyfriend take his life in front of her

R&B Singer Mary J. Blige experienced divorce, addiction and multiple heartbreaks

Rapper Jay Z experienced poverty and was labeled a statistic

Rapper Kanye West experienced the loss of his mother

Soulful singer Whitney Houston experienced addiction

Michael Jackson experienced low self-esteem and social acceptance

Elvis Presley experienced identity crisis

Comedian Robin Williams experienced depression

Nelson Mandela experienced racism and severe punishment

Shirley Chisolm experienced prejudice

Barack Obama experienced prejudice

Jesus Christ experienced the crucifixion

I, _____ (Insert Your Name Here) have

experienced_____

_____

_____   _____

In order to be great; be a boss and make boss moves you must
be willing to pay the price. Being successful may seem glamorous
to many but those who truly experience it knows that it comes
with great sacrifice and submission.

5 Steps to Living the Life of Your Dream

1. **You must be honest about what it is you want-**
Once you have identified your heart's desire, go to
God in prayer and ask for HIS heart's desire. Don't
waste your life doing what's comfortable or safe (I am
not referring to anything illegal but more so anything
that keeps you within your comfort zone.)

   You are going to experience pain anyway so why not
   benefit from it? Each of the individuals mentioned
   above transformed their pain into power by using their
   story as fuel for their passion which ultimately led to
   their life purpose.

   In Psalm 27:4, David says, "One thing have I desired
   of the Lord, that I will seek after. That I may dwell in
   the house of the Lord all the days of my life, to behold
   the beauty of the Lord and to inquire in his temple."

True inner peace comes from obedience to God. When you and I make a conscious decision to disobey God, we cancel out our own future. Now sure you can live a very successful life according to the world's standards but the good book asks a question: What does it profit a man to gain the whole world yet in return lose his soul.

Money can't be your number one driving force when it comes to living the life of your dreams. Your dream life should be centered-around living a life that pleases Christ. This my friend is revealed through prayer, fasting and seeking wise counsel to bring clarity to the things that Holy Spirit is revealing to you.

2. **You must be willing to do the work (pay the price)** - Proverbs 10:4 says lazy hands make for poverty but diligent hands bring wealth.

If you desire to be successful you are going to have to work for it especially if you do not desire to take the traditional path to success which includes a 9 to 5.

When you are pursuing your dream everything will come up against you but it is not to make you quit but to help you soar higher above all the madness. This goes back to the power of perception. How you perceive a matter exposes your ability to allow it to either cause you to quit or dig deeper.

3. **You must be willing to GROW up in order to GO up-** To live the life of your dreams it will not only require maturity but also focus. There will be many things in life that will demand your focus and attention but you have the power to choose where your focus will go.

   Allow trials of life to mature you and cause you to think bigger and dream higher rather than cause you to drown in depression.

   Spiritual maturity comes through passing tests when tempted to quit and go the easy route.

4. **You must develop tough skin-** I'm sure you have heard the saying, "Stop crying over spilled milk." Meaning: It happened. Now what are you going to do about it. Are you going to allow what has happened to you to make you better or cause you to be stuck and better?

   Sadly, very few choose the first option because it causes for you to face what happened and work through your issues.

   In developing tough skin you must learn how to ignore what others think of you soar further into purpose. I like to say, if people aren't talking then you aren't doing much.

In contrast to that, if you can hear everything the naysayers are whispering then you are tuned into the wrong frequency. I encourage you to change the station to Purpose Channel.

Surround yourself with people who will correct and challenge you but are careful not to degrade you in the process. This will take maturity and tough skin in order to handle.

5. **You must put God back in the driver seat of your life-** As Kingdom men and women we operate off of a different frequency. We are accustomed to taking the high road which unfortunately is the road less traveled. Remember that God is the CEO of your life (contrary to what many teach today and you are the COO.

The Chief Executive Officer (CEO) is the one who gives the orders. You receive these through prayer and studying the Word of God which equals having a relationship with Him and not just some religious experience.

The Chief Operating Officer (COO) is the one who follows out the orders given by the CEO. Simply put: Do what God says, the way He says it, when he says it and with whom he says and watch everything work out for your good.

If you are been trying to do it all on your own let today be the day that you get out of the driver seat and give

God the keys to drive your car of purpose while you be a good passenger, taking notes and relying on him to lead and guide you throughout the process.

Complete the below portion and then cut it out and place it somewhere you can view daily to serve as a reminder of your new commitment.

MY COMMITMENT:

I, _____ (Insert Your Name Here) make a cognizant decision to get out of the driver seat and I turn my keys over to Jesus. God I admit I have been trying to do this all on my own and it has led to doubt, burnout and frustration. The vision I have is from you and I trust you for the provision. No longer will I try to do anything in my own strength but I lean and depend totally on you trusting you. God I give you my life; do with it what you may. Lead me, guide me and show me the way. This is my commitment to you, myself and my family. I want to be used for your glory. Show me how to be a Kingdom BOSS man or woman that you have predestined me to be. I submit to your way. I surrender to your will. I relinquish unto you total control.

Signed: _____

(Insert Your Signature Here)

Chapter 7

LEVEL UP YOUR BRAND

Do you currently operate or desire to run your own business? If you answered yes to either question I wrote this portion of the book for you.

There was nothing special about me that enabled me to fire my boss by the age of 30. I simply had the drive, commitment and faith to pursue in life what I spoke out of my mouth that I wanted.

Sadly, not enough people's walk match their talk. Many talk a good game but very few can walk it out on a consistent basis; which led to me writing this book.

Often times I see too many people place their dreams on a shelf because a love one dies, they get fired from their job, their spouse wants a divorce, they get pregnant; etc.

Despite the opposition, nothing is worth quitting or no longer pursuing your dream because it gets hard. Is it supposed to be easy? Absolutely not! If it was then everyone would be doing it! Unfortunately some people like being comfortable and playing life safe while others like you and I decide to take chances called risks and trust that we are following our gut (or inner Holy Ghost as I call it) and trust God to lead us where he desires us to go.

In this portion I want to share with you how to level up your brand which simply means how to get from where you are to the next phase in your business as an entrepreneur.

These principles can be applied whether you are an emerging or established entrepreneur or even if you don't desire to be an entrepreneur these principles can be applied to our overall life.

The top 3 reasons most people give for not living the life of their dreams is:

1. A lack of finances
2. Not enough time
3. Client attraction

The #1 proven reason most people do not live the life of their dreams is due to a poor mindset rather than a lack of skillset.

Many have the skill set to do whatever they desire to do but lack the mindset to compliment that gift.

Successful people have a predetermined mindset to win regardless the turbulence they experience in life which we covered earlier.

7 Ways to Level Up Your Brand

1. **Keep your brand fun, fresh and exciting-** No one wants to be too predictable. Give your supporters

something new to copy. To remain relevant switch it up every once in a while. Switch up your style which includes your hair, nails and attire. Add a new feature to your website or release a new product during a certain time frame while effectively marketing it.

The key is to have fun while doing it. Do not allow anyone to put you in a box. Being a Kingdom Entrepreneur is all about being your true, authentic self and allowing people to get the real you.

2. **Don't get too comfortable-** Established entrepreneurs tend to suffer with this one while getting too relaxed and not staying ten steps ahead of the game. Sure, people want someone they can relate to but they also want someone who is where they desire to be. Aspiring and emerging entrepreneurs tend to get stuck in the preparation stage without ever executing. Don't get comfortable preparing. Step out of your comfort zone and take the risk by presenting your idea to the world. Do not allow your fear of feedback to keep you stuck and stagnant. You'll never know you can until you try.

3. **Quitting must never become an option for you-** Sadly too many quit before ever giving their ideas time to flourish. View your vision as a baby: you must birth it, nurture it and then watch it grow up. Continue to gain knowledge by expanding the books you read,

places you congregate and the people you network with. Be careful not to quit prematurely.

4. **Never compare but congratulate-** Jealously and envy is at an all-time high in the marketplace and is killing a lot of visions and minimizing the level of impact we can make when we come together. If one can chase a thousand and two can put two thousand to flight, then why do we continue to try to do it on our own? Embrace your uniqueness, study and perfect your craft and then connect with like-minded individuals who can help sharpen you along the way and you can do the same unto them.

Become well versed in your industry and celebrate others who are well versed in theirs.

If you are in the same industry look at what is being done well and identify if anything is missing and apply it in your brand. Do this all while celebrating, not hating on others. Jealousy and envy is definitely not the garments a Kingdom Boss man or woman should wear.

5. **Surround yourself with winners-** We become the sum total of who we spend the majority of our time with. Sure, we want to adopt this save the world mentality but be careful because those infected tend to rub off on those of who have been cured. Before you know it you too will be lazy, sitting back eating

popcorn while watching Empire rather than building your own.

6. **Consistently renew your mind-** This will require spending time in the Word of God. With so many things to influence the way we think and how we do business, be careful never to get away from the core of who you are. Who we really are is who we are in the spirit.

7. **Keep God as your CEO-** As Kingdom entrepreneurs it is essential that we know our set place in our business. Although you may get the itch to prove to everyone that you are not a failure, unstoppable and can win at life but that will drain you of your energy and infect your motive to please God. Instead of wasting energy on proving your naysayers wrong, redirect that energy to operating in excellence and showing God that he can trust you with the work he has placed in your hands to do while in the earth. We only have a limited amount of time here, therefore, let's make it count!

Chapter 8

BOSS ELEVATOR PITCH

An elevator pitch can be defined as a brief, persuasive speech that you use to spark interest in what your organization does. You can also use them to create interest in a project, idea, or product – or in yourself. A good elevator pitch should last no longer than a short elevator ride of 20 to 30 seconds, hence the name.

Often times in business many shy away from networking events because they dread being asked this single question: *"What do you do?"*

Within Trailblazers Coaching Academy I share with my students (learn more at www.trailblazerscoaching.org) how to create what I call a BOSS Elevator Pitch which helps you describe briefly what it is that you do in an energetic and appealing manner without leaving you in sweats and a racing heartbeat.

An elevator pitch should sound natural, authentic and be straight and to the point.

In the example provided below I want you to practice using this in your business or whatever your life purpose is when you are asked what it is that you do.

It is natural to feel nervous about introducing yourself & sharing about your business. But in order to excel as a Kingdom Entrepreneur it is crucial that you become comfortable with the gifts God has blessed you with by sharing the services & solutions you provide. I encourage you to print this document, fill in the blanks & then re-write this on a note card and recite it daily until it becomes natural (a part of you.) With much practice & preparation you'll be delivering a BOSS Elevator Pitch in no time!

To better serve you I have included my responses in parenthesis.

I am _____
(A Breakthrough Strategist & Trainer) **and what I do is**

_____

_____

_____

(I help aspiring entrepreneurs break through the barriers of where they are currently in an effort to reposition and equip them to begin to dream with their eyes wide open while building a lucrative brand.)

I do this by way of

_____

_____

(Of books, training courses as well as both live and virtual events.)

My targeted audience is/are

_____

_____

(Those who have an idea of what they desire to do, but lack directives on how to walk it out.)

After you have completed the above begin reciting it aloud daily until it becomes natural and a part of who you are so when you share it you come across as authentic rather than robotic.

One of the things I disliked about networking events was there seemed to be very few authentic connections made because everyone came across as trying to pitch their business to me.

Be careful not to speak to those you meet as if they are potential clients (although some may be). This can be viewed as a turn off although you may walk away with tons of business cards with no true connections being made.

Tips for Attending Networking Events:

1. Identify your purpose & #1 goal for attending: If you are attending to meet potential clients then that is fine and let that be your focus but ensure the event is targeted toward your audience or it will be a waste of time.

2. Smile- Be warm and inviting.

3. Be careful not to talk about yourself too much- I've had this happen to the point the woman would not shut up and I had to pretend I received a phone call

just to get away from her. You do not want to be this person.

4. Research the event prior to attending- Never attend an event without researching what caliber of people will be attending.

5. Have fun- Connecting with others should be fun and is a part of being a Kingdom BOSS. Treat everyone with the upmost respect for you never know who they are or how they can help you transition from your now to your next!

Chapter 9

BRANDING LIKE BEYONCÉ

You literally have to be living under a rock not to know who R&B Mogul, Beyoncé is. She is the founding leader of the girl group, Destiny's Child (American girl group that consisted of Kelly Rowland, Michelle Williams and of course Beyoncé). She is also a wife and mother of three beautiful babies. She is a singer and actress Her net worth is considered to be over $350 million however, simply put, she is a woman who had a dream and went for it!

The reason I named this chapter Branding Like Beyoncé is because she spent years making a name for herself and although she has made the news headlines throughout her career you don't find her responding too much to criticism regarding her marriage or career.

Beyoncé is a young woman in her mid-thirties whom a lot of women have watched grow up right before our eyes as a mainstream artist. Not only is she iconic but she did something no other artist is known for doing and that was without any marketing or promotions she announces her new album in December 2013 at midnight and instantly fans rushed to iTunes to purchase it. Within three days she sold over 617,000 records worldwide breaking the U.S. iTunes sales record.

She was able to do this without any pre-release announcement. During this time she beat out Taylor Swift's album which sold 465,000 in the week of October 2012. Beyoncé's album debuted at Number 1 on the Billboard charts.

Why am I sharing all of this? To show that hard work always pays off. Beyoncé began singing at an early age and her mother was her stylist while her father was her manager and through various turbulent experiences she continued to soar and use all of the hate, gossip and lies as momentum.

You my friend will have to do the same thing if you desire to win in whatever industry you are called to.

In my book, *The Entrepreneur Blueprint* (Grab your copy at www.CarlaCannon.com) I share that branding is how you get known and this is determined by the content you put out and how you live your life.

The world is a lot smaller than it seems and everyone seems to know everyone therefore, bad news travels fast although good news often seems to travel at a slower pace.

In the midst of it all Beyoncé did not quit. Earlier in her career she went through staff changes with two members of her group: LaTavia and LeToya but guess what? Her and bff, Kelly Rowland did not quit. They later decided to add Michelle Williams to the group and went on to become one of the most popular female R&B groups of the late 90s.

It wasn't until 2002 when Beyoncé's solo recording was a feature on rapper Jay Z's (her now husband) song: "Bonnie &

Clyde" that peaked at number four on the U.S. Billboard Hot 100 chart.

Her first solo album was Dangerously in Love which released in 2003. It has been over fourteen years since she went solo and she doesn't appear to be stopping anytime soon.

She married Jay Z in 2008 however, in 2004 there was an issue in an elevator between her, hubby Jay Z and sister Solange. However, it took years for either of them to respond.

As you can imagine Jay Z referenced the incident in his latest album that dropped in 2017 entitled, 4:44 which was many fans seemed to be waiting for.

Beyoncé is known for addressing rumors in her music but only for those who have a keen ear to recognize it. She sent many fans off with her "Lemonade" album when she referenced "Becky with the good hair."

With this being said, what can we learn from Beyoncé as it relates to branding?

1. **You set the tone for your career:** How you brand yourself is important and will follow you throughout your life therefore, be careful the books you write, content you reveal, events you attend and public views and nonsense you post on social media. It could come back to haunt you.

2. **Put your energy into your work-** Beyoncé mentioned one time that she was so focused on her work that she forgot to eat. Now I am not encouraging you to do this but rather use it as ammunition or encouragement to go hard and go after the life you say you want.

3. **Keep the main thing the main thing-** In the midst of criticism Beyoncé continues to win. Her motives, religion, character and even her marriage have been questioned but it has not stopped Queen Bey (as the world calls her), neither should you allow it to stop you.

4. **Give people what they want-** Do this but control how it is distributed. Sure, Beyoncé has troubles like anyone else but she controls where and when she responds and it always ends up being profitable on her end.

5. **Build Your Social Media Presence-** Regardless of the industry you are in being on social media puts you in front of people and gives them an opportunity to connect with you but again you control the content you put out and how much of your life you desire to share. As I scroll through Beyoncé's Instagram page that has over 107 million followers I notice she shares graphics that compliment her brand/personality as well as photos with her family. One thing to keep in mind when building your social media presence is knowing your audience and what they want to see. People

around the world purchase Beyoncé's music and follow her on social media because they like what she represents and feels in one way or another whether through her music or story that they can relate to her. That's the key. Ensure your brand and content is relatable. Don't post for likes but do pay attention to what type of posts gain the most traction and give your supporters more of that.

Building your online presence takes time, strategy and consistency especially if you desire to build your list organically. Whether you have 5 followers or 500 give them the authentic you and those who your message is for will be attracted to that just as many are attracted to Beyoncé's brand.

This portion of the book is by no means to promote Beyoncé's brand as I could have chosen anyone around the world to use however, I found her to be one that was relatable to my target audience who will read this book.

As we bring this portion of the book to a close I encourage you to review your notes and highlights and be sure to apply them to your brand, business and overall life.

Be careful not to allow this to be another book you speed through without catching the many valuable principles and values that were shared.

Chapter 10

WHAT'S NEXT?

If anything I said within the pages of this book resonated with you I would love the opportunity to better serve you if

- You are interested in learning how to break the endless cycle of defeat off your life and tap into abundance now!

- You are eager to learn how to position yourself to dream with your eyes wide open!

- If you are ready to fire your boss but are unsure of the next steps of transitioning into full time entrepreneurship.

- If you are ready to awaken your inner boss!

Want to connect further?

I'd love to become your Breakthrough Coach and have the opportunity to assist you in entering the next phase of your life! Because you took the time to read this book I'd like to extend to you a FREE 15 minute strategy session in which we can see how I can better serve you as you on your path to awakening your inner boss.

To schedule your complimentary strategy session with me send an email to: Admin@womenofstandard.org with "Awaken Your Inner Boss FREE Strategy Session" in the subject line or call my office at 888-502-2228.

Connect with me on social media:

Twitter: @CarlaRCannon

Facebook: Carla R Cannon (Public Figure Page)

Periscope: @CarlaRCannon

Lastly, if you have read this book and you feel your inner boss has been awakened I want you to go to your Twitter account and type: *"Carla, my inner boss has been awakened! I'm ready for the next step!"* Be sure to use the hashtag #bossmoves & tag me if you can!

After you do this, email me and we can get started immediately! Remember this is only for those of you who don't mind being stretched, gut/cut out and birthed into your purpose! I am also a coach to many other coaches and leadership and development is the core of my brand. I would love the opportunity to become your Breakthrough Coach!

Now, that you have been awakened don't you dare go back to sleep!

ABOUT THE AUTHOR

Carla R. Cannon also known as "The Trailblazer" is indeed one of *God's Moguls* in the making. With her eloquent yet transparent approach she is committed to empowering global women from the pulpit to the marketplace on how to operate authentically and un-apologetically in their divine calling with a spirit of excellence.

Carla is a mother, National Best Selling Author, Conference Host and Entrepreneur who currently resides in North Carolina. One of the key areas Carla specializes in is teaching others how to profit from their pain by developing their storm into a story and their mess into a movement. Carla currently runs and operates Carla R. Cannon Enterprises which houses Cannon Publishing where she has currently assisted numerous men and women on how to Write the Book Already and produce multiple streams of income to provide for their families.

Carla is also the leader of a global brand, *Women of Standard*, where her mission is to make Jesus famous and in an effort in doing so she is currently on tour.

The testimony of this young woman of faith and her ability to share her story unashamed and with such boldness and conviction is truly what causes her to connect with others on multiple levels. Whether she is speaking to an audience of 1 or 1,000 the energy Carla exudes is magnetic, and contagious for she always leaves her audience not only feeling hopeful but with the tools to pursue their dreams and move further into their path of purpose. She is truly a woman after God's own heart and lives her life not trying to correct all of her wrongs but to learn and grow from them daily.

Carla has been privileged to be featured on multiple radio talk shows including The Jewel Tankard Show (featuring Jewel Tankard from the hit show, *Thicker Than Water*.) Carla has also shared the stage with many prominent leaders such as Dr. Yvonne Capehart, Real Talk Kim, Jekalyn Carr, Tera C. Hodges, Dr. Jamal Bryant and many more!

In 2014 Carla was invited to cover media for Bishop T. D. Jakes' annual Woman Thou Art Loosed Conference where tens of thousands of women and men assembled together. Carla's message is simple: *No matter what you are in, you can come out and recover ALL!*

Book Carla for Your Next Event!

Are you planning an upcoming conference, retreat, workshop or beyond and are seeking a speaker who is knowledgeable, relatable, and transparent? Consider booking Carla for your upcoming conference.

Carla's area of focus is on the personal development and growth of others. Having her as your conference speaker is sure to leave your audience UNLOCKED, UNLEASHED & ACTIVATED!

Some of her speaking topics include (but are not limited to):

I.   Defining the Pearl In You- Teaching women about self-love, self-worth and spiritual development.

II. Write Like a BOSS- During this boot camp style training, Carla shares the exact step by step process which led to the success of her writing career in which she has written & published 8 internationally best-selling books!

III. Unlock, Unleash & Activate!- This is Carla's signature message where she shares how individuals can unlock hidden or untapped potential, unleash their God-given gifts and activate into their divine calling and set place of purpose!

For booking information please visit
http://carlacannon.com/book-carla/ or call 888-502-2228.

Sample Events Carla has Spoken At:

Do you desire to write a book?

Check out Carla's current training manual entitled, Write the Book Already to learn how you can write a book to launch your business!

This step by step guide has helped hundreds across the globe share their story and life experiences with eloquence, intention and purpose.

Visit http://carlacannon.com/write-book-already-writers-coaching-program/ to get started today!

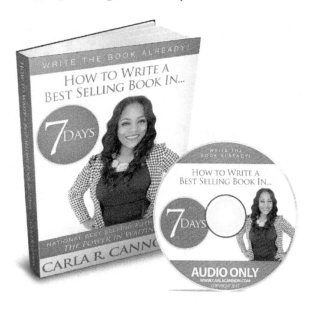

Are You Seeking A Publisher?

CHARMIN Y. ANDERSON

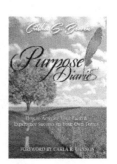

WWW.CANNONPUBLISHING.NET

Made in the USA
Columbia, SC
03 August 2021

42622065R00046